THE RAILROAD
IN AMERICAN HISTORY

THE RAILROAD FUELS WESTWARD EXPANSION
(1870s)

Russell Roberts

Mitchell Lane
PUBLISHERS

P.O. Box 196
Hockessin, Delaware 19707

THE RAILROAD

IN AMERICAN HISTORY

The Birth of the Locomotive
The Railroad Comes to America
The Railroad Grows into an Industry
The Railroad and the Civil War
The Railroad Fuels Westward Expansion
Electric Trains and Trolleys

The publisher would like to thank Milton C. Hallberg for acting as a consultant on its *The Railroad in American History* series. He is a professor emeritus of agricultural economics at Pennsylvania State University and has been a visiting professor at universities around the world. His railroad interests began when he attended a railroad telegraphers' school in preparation for a job as a depot agent on the CB&Q Railroad in Illinois. After retiring from teaching, he returned to his railroad interests as a new hobby, during which time he has written about early rail systems.

PUBLISHER'S NOTE:
The facts on which this book is based have been thoroughly researched. Documentation of such research can be found on page 44. While every possible effort has been made to ensure accuracy, the publisher will not assume liability for damages caused by inaccuracies in the data, and makes no warranty on the accuracy of the information contained herein.

Printing
1   2   3   4   5   6   7   8   9

Library of Congress Cataloging-in-Publication Data
Roberts, Russell, 1953-
  The railroad fuels westward expansion (1870s) / by Russell Roberts.
    p. cm. —(The railroad in American history)
  Includes bibliographical references and index.
  ISBN 978-1-61228-290-9 (library bound)
  1. Railroads--United States—History—19th century—Juvenile literature. 2. Pacific railroads—Juvenile literature. 3. United States--Territorial expansion—Juvenile literature. I. Title.
  TF23.R63 2013
  385.0973'09034—dc23
                                        2012009424

eBook ISBN: 9781612283647

PLB

CONTENTS

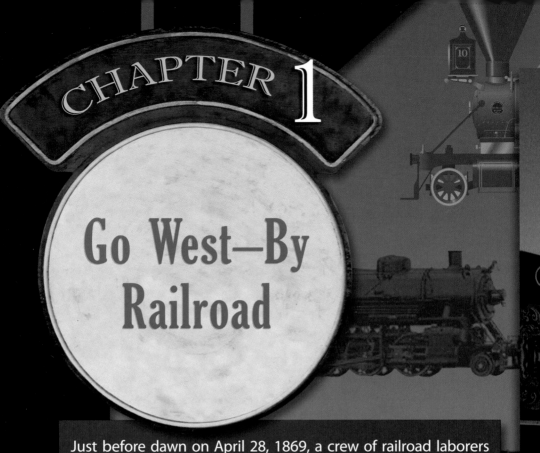

CHAPTER 1

Go West—By Railroad

Just before dawn on April 28, 1869, a crew of railroad laborers waited impatiently for the whistle to begin one of the strangest races ever recorded.

It was not a race in the normal sense—runners racing for a finish line. Rather, it was a race to see how many miles of track these men could lay in one day. The crew was from the Union Pacific Railroad construction company, and they were one of two groups building the transcontinental railroad, the epic railroad line that was going to span the United States and make travel to the West Coast quick and easy. Both they and the Central Pacific Railroad Company had been building the rail line for several years—the Union Pacific heading from Nebraska to the west, and the Central Pacific going from California to the east—and the two were to join their lines together at Promontory Summit in Utah. Today, however, was all about the money.

The money in question was a $10,000 bet between Charles Crocker of the Central Pacific and the Union Pacific's Thomas

Promontory Summit in Utah today, with a re-creation of the scene on that May day in 1869 when trains from both lines met, signaling the completion of the transcontinental railroad and the beginning of the transformation of the United States.

The workers that laid the track for the transcontinental railroad were a hard lot, and they had to be. The job was tough and tedious, requiring hours of back-breaking labor outside in all types of weather.

Durant. Durant's men had been laying track at an incredible clip, and in October 1868 he challenged Crocker to prove that his construction crews were faster. Crocker accepted the bet, saying that his men could lay down ten miles (sixteen kilometers) of track in one day—an unheard-of pace that no one thought possible. Now the time had come to see if he was right, or had just been bragging.

As dawn broke a whistle shrieked, cutting through the chilly half-light of morning, signaling the start of the contest. A locomotive with sixteen packed cars of supplies—iron rails, kegs of spikes, rail connectors called fish plates, and more—sat on the tracks where they had ended the previous night. When the whistle sounded a large group of Chinese laborers leaped onto the cars and began unloading them at incredible speed. Within eight minutes, every car was stripped bare and the train was backing onto a side track to make room for the next one.

Next, six men lifted small flatcars called iron cars onto the track and loaded each of them with sixteen rails, plus all the hardware needed to lay down new track. Two horses with riders were hitched to each car. At the same time men aligned the wooden crossties that had been placed on the ground and waited for the iron rails to connect them.

The first flatcar raced up to the end of the previously laid tracks. There, eight big, burly Irish laborers stood waiting to unload the rails, while other men waited to grab the hardware kegs and other items. The instant the flatcar slowed the Irish workers grabbed the rails and threw them down, using a portable track gauge to make sure that each rail was the right distance from the other rail. The rails were then attached to the crossties.

This process was repeated over and over: loaded flatcar arriving, rails and hardware unloaded and thrown down, connectors and spikes pounded in. The men moved with military precision, like the gears of a well-oiled machine. Crocker had promised each man four days' wages if they were successful, so the laborers had as much riding on the challenge as their boss.

Throughout the morning the construction crews worked, and witnesses were astonished to see that the tracks were being laid down almost as fast as a man could walk. A Union Pacific representative timed the rate at an amazing 240 feet (73 meters) of track every 80 seconds.[1] As the construction crews moved relentlessly forward, they were shadowed by teams hauling food and water wagons. Chinese workers carrying water and tea on the ends of long poles balanced over their shoulders also moved rapidly up and down the line.

The pace was amazing—impossible to believe, and by mid-morning several miles of track had been laid. Whether the breakneck pace could be sustained was doubtful. The rails alone were 30 feet (9 meters) long and weighed around 560 pounds. How long could the eight Irish laborers keep lifting them? How long could any of the men keep up this grueling pace?

The goal was ten miles (sixteen kilometers) of track laid down in one day—was it impossible?

End of the Line

The transcontinental railroad was the end result of a quest that had begun a half-century before.

In 1800, just a few years after the United States became an independent nation, it was so hard to get from one place to the other that political leaders worried the union of states would not survive.[2] More than two-thirds of the U.S. population of 5 million people lived within 50 miles (80 kilometers) of the Atlantic Ocean. People who lived in the interiors of states might as well have been living on another planet. New England was isolated from the Middle Atlantic, the Middle Atlantic from the South, and so on. America was all one country, but it was all very separate.

People who journeyed long distances usually traveled by water. They sailed up and down the Atlantic coast, or they used canoes, rafts, and other types of boats to travel on rivers throughout the interior of the country. There were few roads, and those were muddy and rutted.

Traveling along these roads in a wagon was unpleasant and painful. A man who traveled to the New Jersey coast in what was called a "Jersey wagon" described how passengers were bounced around furiously and feasted upon by flies and other insects. By the end of the journey, said the man, "the more robust were generally able to climb out [of the wagon] but the feebler ones . . . had to be lifted out."[3]

It was just as difficult to move freight. The nation's merchants needed a better way to get their goods to market, but how?

At first canals were considered the answer to America's transportation woes. The manmade channels dug between two bodies of water promised to solve a lot of problems. The states hurried to build canals, and by 1830 several thousand miles of them had been approved throughout the country.[4] However, the water in them froze in winter and

Before the railroad, canals were thought to be the answer to America's transportation problem. However, after some were built, like the Erie Canal, the limitations of water transportation became all too clear.

the maintenance costs were high. Clearly another type of transportation system was needed.

Railroads were already operating in several states east of the Mississippi River, including New York and Maryland. However, there was little interest in trying to construct a railroad over the 1,600 miles (2,500 kilometers) from Missouri to California. Most people thought the railroad was only useful for covering short distances.[5]

Not everyone had such a limited view of the railroad. In 1832, Dr. Hartwell Carver of Rochester, New York, published a series of articles in which he called for a transcontinental railroad to be built. In 1838, Welsh immigrant John Plumbe sent a petition to Congress advocating a transcontinental railroad. People ridiculed Plumbe and said his request was as silly as asking the government "to build a railroad to the moon."[6]

Some people did not believe that a railroad across the West was worth it. Others, like merchant Asa Whitney, believed otherwise, and men such as he gradually convinced others of the soundness of their arguments.

In 1844, merchant Asa Whitney began promoting a scheme for a transcontinental railroad that was "build as you go." He wanted to finance the building of a railroad as he went along, with profits made from selling the surrounding land upon which he had just built tracks. The scheme failed, but Whitney succeeded in starting a dialogue about the need for a transcontinental railroad.

Others, such as Massachusetts Senator Daniel Webster, believed the reported dangers were not worth the risk. In 1845, Webster asked, "What do we want with this region [the West] of savages and wild beasts, of deserts, of shifting sands and whirlwinds of dust, of cactus and prairie dogs? What could we do with the western coast line three thousand miles away, rockbound, cheerless and uninviting?"[7]

Americans knew exactly what they wanted to do with the West. Manifest Destiny—the idea that the United States should control all the land from the Atlantic to the Pacific—was sweeping the country. Many Americans were heading west, seeking new land to farm, new places to live—a fresh start. The taming of the West became the great American

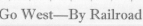

dream, especially when the United States gained territory from Mexico after the Mexican-American War (1846–1848). When gold was discovered in California in 1848, a floodgate opened and even more people poured west.

A trip to California was hazardous and hard. By wagon overland from Missouri—where the wilderness began—it took five months to reach the Pacific coast. Along the way, pioneers had to contend with foul weather, angry Native Americans, disease, food and water shortages, and equipment breakdowns. By sea it also took five months; a ship had to sail all the way around the tip of South America and then head up the coast to San Francisco. Besides enduring foul weather and spoiled food, passengers risked drowning if the ship sank. The journey could be made shorter by sailing to Central America and traveling by land across the Isthmus of Panama, but the route was through hot, humid tropical conditions where the threat of catching deadly yellow fever was extremely high. Clearly, another method of reaching the West Coast was needed.

Meanwhile the railroad was gaining momentum in the United States. From just 23 miles (37 kilometers) of working railroad track in 1830, the nation had more than 9,000 miles (14,500 kilometers) of working track by 1850.[8] People were realizing that the railroad was the transportation mode of the future.

Then a man named Theodore Judah came onto the scene.

He was a railroad surveyor who worked for the emerging Sacramento Valley Railroad. He confidently predicted that a transcontinental railroad was a certainty. His boundless enthusiasm for the idea earned him the nickname of "Crazy Judah." People scoffed at the prospect of a railroad finding a passageway through the towering Sierra Nevada range, which was 400 miles (650 kilometers) long and had peaks as high as 14,000 feet (4,250 meters). As Judah was searching for a way through, he received a letter from California storekeeper Daniel "Doc" Strong, who suggested he look at Donner Pass. When Judah did, he knew he had

If there was one man who could be said to be the "father" of the transcontinental railroad, it was Theodore Judah. Sadly, he did not live to see his dream transformed into reality.

found the way for his railroad through the mountains. He also strongly pushed for the Mormon Trail to be selected as the railroad's route.

Judah gathered California investors for the project, known as the Big Four: Collis Huntington, Mark Hopkins, Leland Stanford, and Charles Crocker. He was so committed to the project that he went to Washington, D.C., to lobby for it. However, Congress and the country at large were preoccupied with the issue that was shortly to plunge the United States into a civil war—slavery. The transcontinental railroad became ensnared in the slavery debate and the growing cries for secession.

Would the transcontinental railroad ever be built?

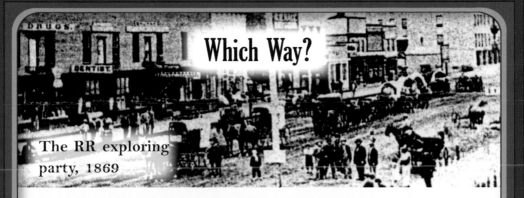

Which Way?

The RR exploring party, 1869

The major way that the proposed transcontinental railroad became trapped in the slavery debate in the U.S. Congress was in the choice of a route.

Five possible routes were under consideration for the railroad:

1. The Northern Trail – This route, 1,854 miles (2,984 kilometers) long, ran from St. Paul, Minnesota, to Vancouver by way of the upper Missouri River. The estimated cost for this route was $117,121,000.

2. The Mormon Trail – So named because it was the route Mormons traveled to go west, it was 2,032 miles (3,270 kilometers) long and ran from Council Bluffs, Iowa, to San Francisco. This cost was estimated at $116,095,000.

3. The Buffalo Trail – It began at Kansas City and ran for 2,080 miles (3,347 kilometers) through the Rocky Mountains before ending at San Francisco. Costs were estimated to be so high as to make this route impossible.

4. The 35th Parallel Trail – This route was only 1,892 miles (3,045 kilometers) long. It ran from Fort Smith, Arkansas, to Los Angeles (then called San Pedro). The estimated cost was $169,210,222.

5. The Southern Trail – Just 1,618 miles (2,604 kilometers), it ran from Fulton, Arkansas, through Texas, New Mexico, and Arizona, and ended at San Diego. Estimated cost: $68,970,000.

Southern leaders pushed for the Southern Trail. They worried that the choice of a northern or even centrally located route for the railroad would result in anti-slavery states being settled. Northerners fought against the Southern Trail, fearing that it would cause California and other western areas to become pro-slavery.

This debate stalled the transcontinental railroad in Congress.

CHAPTER 2

Spanning a Continent

It seemed for a time that the transcontinental railroad was going to get waylaid by the furor over slavery. Once the Southern states began seceding from the Union to join the Confederacy, Southern congressmen resigned from Congress. This opened the door for the remaining congressional members to select the route for the railroad. They chose the Mormon Trail.

On July 1, 1862, President Abraham Lincoln signed the Pacific Railroad Act. Lincoln had worked with railroads as an attorney before he became president. He believed that the existence of a transcontinental railroad would help unify the country. The legislation called for the Central Pacific Railroad Company to lay track east from Sacramento, California, and the Union Pacific Railroad Company to lay track west from the Missouri River. For each mile of track laid, a company would be granted 640 acres of adjoining land. The government also lent the companies $16,000 for each mile of track laid in flatlands, $32,000 for each mile in foothills,

A statue of Lincoln outside Springfield Union Station in Springfield, Illinois

and $48,000 for each mile in the mountains.[1] However, the companies would forfeit all land and monies if they did not finish the railroad in twelve years.

On January 8, 1863, the Central Pacific Railroad broke ground in Sacramento, California. The groundbreaking ceremonies for the Union Pacific were held on December 2, 1863, in Omaha in the Nebraska Territory.

Coming in the midst of the Civil War that had shattered America, both Lincoln and others hoped that the railroad would tie the diverse sections of the country together.

"When this shall have been done disunion will be rendered forever after impossible," said Secretary of State William Seward. "There will be no fulcrum for the lever of treason to rest upon."[2]

The railroad did not get off to a flying start. The Civil War was like a giant sinkhole, sucking both men and materials into it. This meant that the transcontinental railroad builders had to scramble for whatever they could get.

Typical of the railroad's problems was one encountered by Theodore Judah. Instructed to buy six locomotives for the Central Pacific Railroad, Judah was only able to buy four. Thanks to the war driving up the demand and price for railroad supplies, Judah paid over 50 percent more for the locomotives than they had cost just two years before.[3]

The Union Pacific was having its own problems. After two years it had built just forty miles (sixty-four kilometers) of track. Its ownership was fragmented, it didn't have enough workers, and it was running out of money.

President Lincoln was dismayed at the Union Pacific's lack of progress. He called millionaire Oakes Ames to his office early in 1865. "Ames, take hold of this," said the President, referring to the railroad. "That road must be built, and you are the only man to do it."[4] Ames helped arrange new financing for the struggling company.

With the Civil War's end in April 1865, thousands of soldiers were suddenly available for work. Freed slaves and men whose way of life had been destroyed by the war also began flooding into Omaha to work on the railroad. Between the new financing and improved labor situation, the tortoise became the hare. The Union Pacific began almost flying across the plains, often laying a mile (1.6 kilometers) of track a day. In 1866, the company laid 266 miles (428 kilometers) of track.[5]

Meanwhile, the Central Pacific was having problems finding workers. The railroad was offering a wage of two or three dollars per day but finding few takers. Most people could earn more than that at easier jobs; besides, many had come to California to seek their fortune in the gold fields, not to work for wages. In early 1865, the company advertised for 5,000 workers to lay track across the foreboding Sierra Nevada Mountains; it got only 200.[6]

At wit's end, Charles Crocker, the general superintendent of the Central Pacific, decided to strike out in a different direction and hire

Chinese workers building
the railroad, 1860s

The Chinese had come to the United States in search of a better life, and to escape strife in their homeland. A great many settled in California, but unfortunately here they encountered poor treatment, racial prejudice, and outright violence.

some Chinese laborers from San Francisco. At first the construction superintendent, James Strobridge, was against the idea. He did not believe the Chinese were strong enough to dig tunnels and move great amounts of rock and earth.

"Did they not build the Chinese Wall [the Great Wall of China], the biggest piece of masonry in the world?"[7] retorted Crocker. Strobridge reluctantly agreed to hire fifty Chinese workers on a trial basis.

At the time there were an estimated 60,000 Chinese living in California.[8] Some had come to escape strife in their homeland; others had come to hunt for gold. However, they were discriminated against in California. They had to pay a personal tax, a hospital tax, a school tax, and a property tax, even though they could not vote, attend public school, or testify in court. Chinese gold-seekers were also forced to pay a miner's tax, a $4 permission tax, and a $2 water tax.

The Chinese laborers quickly proved to be tireless workers and resourceful builders on the railroad. They took few breaks, proved adept at using blasting materials, were reliable, and worked for less money

than their white counterparts. The Chinese had to provide their own food and tents in which to live—both perks that white laborers received—yet they rarely complained.

The Chinese stayed remarkably healthy, possibly because of their diet and possibly because they drank only tea poured from small kegs while the other workers all drank from the same pail of dank water with the same dipper. They also hardly ever drank whiskey, did not usually fight or argue, and were honest and extremely clean.

Soon the Central Pacific had hired every Chinese worker they could find, and the railroad president, Leland Stanford, was trying to bring 15,000 more from China. By the summer of 1865, it is estimated that of the 4,000 men at work for the Central Pacific, nine-tenths were Chinese.[9]

However, finding workers was just half the problem. Building this type of line, away from normal supply avenues for materials, was a new experience. Materials for the Central Pacific had to be brought by ship around South America and then up the west coast—a tremendously costly and time-consuming process. Then there was always the danger of materials getting destroyed at sea or even while being unloaded from ships. A locomotive named the *Governor Sanford* traveled nearly 19,000 miles (30,500 kilometers) to the coast by boat, only to be almost lost when it nearly fell into the sea while being unloaded.

The Union Pacific didn't have it any easier. Initially all of its materials had to be brought by ship up the unpredictable Missouri River to Omaha—again, an expensive and time-consuming journey full of danger.

However, the companies managed to find both men and materials, and in the years after the Civil War both laid track at a brisk clip, sometimes several miles per day. It became a race; each company not only wanted to beat the other for competitive reasons, but also so they could qualify for more government bonds and land grants. Soon the companies were approaching each other like long distance runners who saw the finish line.

Then came the great track-laying challenge of April 28, 1869. As the day progressed, the question that hung unanswered in the air was a simple one: Could the Central Pacific workers keep going?

At 1:30 in the afternoon on that day the whistle blew for lunch; six miles (ten kilometers) of track had already been laid. The exhausted workers were grateful for the break. Yet so confident were they of making the record, they all took the full, allotted hour for lunch.

When lunch was over the workers resumed as if they had never stopped. The rails began falling again at a relentless pace, and it soon became apparent that the Central Pacific was going to make the ten-mile (sixteen-kilometer) target.

At dusk the whistle blew again, signaling the end of the workday—and what a remarkable workday it had been. The Central Pacific workers had put down 10 miles 56 feet (16.11 kilometers) of track. They had laid 3,520 rails and sledge-hammered more than 28,000 spikes. To prove that the track was sound, a heavy locomotive passed over it at forty miles (sixty-four kilometers) per hour without a hitch.

"It was just like an army marching over the ground and leaving a track built behind them. . . . " Crocker said of that memorable day.[10]

The workers on the transcontinental railroad faced numerous dangers. Attacks by Native Americans or wild animals were always a risk for work crews. The use of blasting materials was highly dangerous. The extremes of the weather—intense heat in summer, bone-chilling cold in the winter—was another problem. During the winter of 1865–1866, some 3,000 Chinese workers lived and labored in tunnels beneath forty-foot (twelve-meter) snowdrifts.[11] Yet the men persevered.

On May 10, 1869, the Union Pacific and Central Pacific railroad lines met at Promontory Summit in Utah. Locomotives from the two companies were brought up near one another. The locomotive for the Union Pacific was *No. 119,* while the Central Pacific's was called the *Jupiter.* The last spikes were tapped into place, and a telegraph operator sent out a message to the entire country: "It is done!"[12]

America was about to be transformed.

Gauging a Railroad

Just because the Pacific Railroad Act had finally been signed, it didn't mean that construction for the transcontinental railroad could begin immediately. A thousand details had to be decided before the first rail could be laid. Perhaps the most significant detail was what gauge to use for the track.

Track gauge—the distance between the inner sides of the heads of the two load-bearing rails—was not standard in 1862. Tradition held that the most popular gauge of 4 feet, 8.5 inches (1.4 meters) was the width between road ruts caused by the wheels of Roman chariots. However, that is almost certainly a legend. British locomotive builder George Stephenson first ran his engines along tracks with a gauge of 4 feet, 8.5 inches (1.4 meters), which he chose because it was similar to the gauge used on tramways in English mines. Soon it was the standard gauge throughout England. American tracks were of various gauges, with southern railroads using a gauge of 5 feet (1.5 meters), and those in the North using 4 feet, 8.5 inches, 5.5 feet (1.7 meters), and even 6 feet (1.8 meters).

Trains that used different track gauges could not go from one track to another. Passengers and cargo had to be unloaded from one train to another—an expensive and time-consuming process. The gauge of the transcontinental railroad had been left to Lincoln to decide. The Central Pacific Railroad wanted him to set it at five feet. That was the width of tracks in California, and there were several existing tracks in the state that the Central Pacific wanted to use.

When officials at the Central Pacific heard that the Secretary of the Interior was going to recommend a gauge of 4 feet, 8.5 inches to Lincoln, they tried to persuade the President to use five feet instead. They even had an expert on railroad gauges make a presentation to Lincoln, singing the praises of five-foot gauge.

On January 21, 1863, Lincoln signed an order stipulating the gauge size at five feet. But within a few days bills were introduced in Congress setting the gauge at 4 feet, 8.5 inches. Congress passed the measure, and Lincoln signed it into law on March 3. Thus the gauge was set, not only for the transcontinental railroad, but also for other major railroads, since they all wanted to be able to connect seamlessly with the transcontinental railroad.

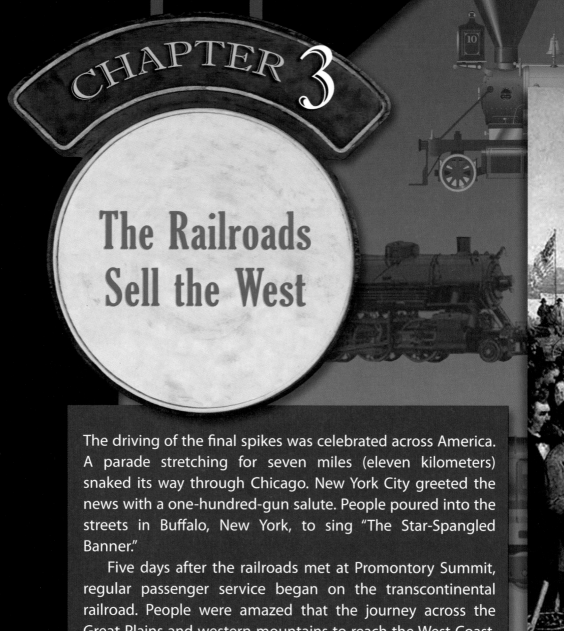

CHAPTER 3

The Railroads Sell the West

The driving of the final spikes was celebrated across America. A parade stretching for seven miles (eleven kilometers) snaked its way through Chicago. New York City greeted the news with a one-hundred-gun salute. People poured into the streets in Buffalo, New York, to sing "The Star-Spangled Banner."

Five days after the railroads met at Promontory Summit, regular passenger service began on the transcontinental railroad. People were amazed that the journey across the Great Plains and western mountains to reach the West Coast, once so difficult and fraught with danger, was now so easy. As *Frank Leslie's Illustrated Newspaper* put it: "The six months' journey is reduced to less than a week. The prairie schooner has passed away, and is replaced by the railway coach with all its modern comforts."[1]

Of course, the trains that now steamed across the West had to be safe to ride, or they would attract far fewer people,

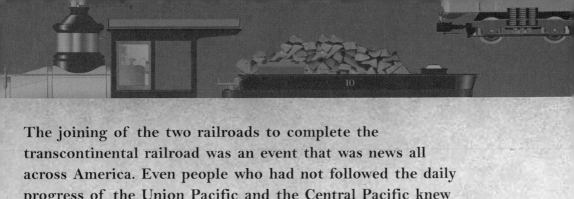

The joining of the two railroads to complete the transcontinental railroad was an event that was news all across America. Even people who had not followed the daily progress of the Union Pacific and the Central Pacific knew that something momentous had just happened, and that the United States was about to be transformed.

no matter how fast they went. One of the biggest safety problems for trains had been braking. However, just as transcontinental travel got going, braking in trains radically improved.

Initially, trains were stopped by steam brakes on the engine and a handbrake on each car. This meant that a brakeman had to ride atop the train and listen for the engineer to blow his whistle to activate the handbrakes (known as "down brakes"). Then the brakeman had to move from car to car and set the brakes by turning a large wheel at the end of each car. If the brakeman didn't hear the whistles or was unable to set all the brakes in time, the result was sometimes a collision or a derailment. It was an imperfect system, and something better was needed.

Something better did indeed come along, just as trains got faster and more powerful and transcontinental travel became a reality. This

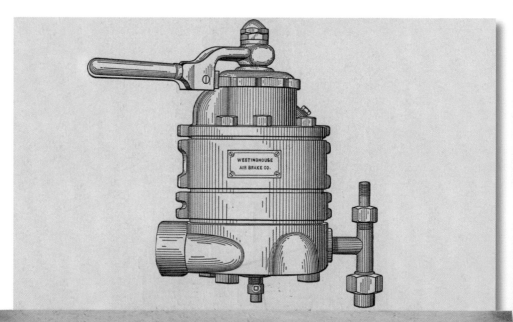

As trains became faster and longer, braking them was a major problem. Westinghouse's air brake was a major improvement over the way braking had previously been done, and was a big reason why people felt safe riding trains.

Even with improved brakes, however, train crashes were still a real possibility because of many other factors, such as bad weather, an obstruction on the track, damaged tracks, and even just plain carelessness on the part of the train crew.

was the air brake, developed by George Westinghouse, who got the idea when he read that tunnel builders were using compressed air to operate drills.

The first Westinghouse air-brake system was patented in 1869. It enabled compressed air from a main reservoir to flow through a system of brake lines connected to each car, and thus activate the brakes. This air-brake system was first used on the *Steubenville Accommodation* running out of Pittsburgh. It stopped the train, which would have hit a farmer's wagon on the tracks if the brakes had been set in the old way.

However, while this system was a major improvement over the former braking method, it had a flaw: If the brake lines for a car were ruptured, the brakes would not work. So Westinghouse revamped the entire system, and in 1872 patented an improved system. This one required each car to carry a supply of compressed air. Moreover, it was designed so that if something happened to the brake lines to signal a decrease in pressure the brakes would automatically go on.

The introduction of air brakes enabled trains to become bigger and faster, as befitted the railroad's new role in settling the United States. Another thing that helped around the same time was the development of steel rails. Steel rails began being used in the United States after 1865, and as the older iron rails wore out, they were replaced with steel ones.

These rails were usually 56-pound or 60-pound rail—meaning the weight of the rail per yard. Whereas iron rails were about 18 feet long (5.5 meters), the early steel rails were 30 feet (9 meters) long. This was a major improvement in rail strength, because the weakest part of the rail is the joint, and longer rails meant fewer joints.

These improvements in safety and power made the transcontinental railroad a lure that few could resist. In 1870, almost 150,000 people took the trip between Omaha, Nebraska, and Sacramento, California.[2]

"Every man who could command the time and money was eager to make the trip [west]," said one rider.[3] And why not? For the price of $100, first-class passengers could speed their way west, riding in nicely decorated train cars featuring steam heat. An extra $4 per day bought meals. Their seats could be converted to sleepers at night (for an additional charge, of course). All the while, porters and conductors bustled up and down the aisles, attending to passengers' every need. It certainly beat crossing the same distance in a rickety covered wagon.

While transporting the curious was fine, the railroads could make money only if the West were settled. Towns had to be built and people convinced to stay. By March 1871, the U.S. government had given more than 170 million acres of land to 80 railroads.[4] The railroads sold it cheaply as an incentive for people to move west for good.

The railroads did their best to hype the West as a Garden of Eden to entice people to come to it. Both the Union Pacific and Central Pacific lines employed photographers to document their construction progress, and they used these photos to help sell the West. Alfred A. Hart, Andrew J. Russell, and others photographed the landscapes through which the tracks were laid. Their photos were reproduced in magazines, newspapers, guidebooks, posters, and many other places.

Typical of the overblown wording that the railroads used to sell the West was this description: "The traveler beholds, stretching away to the distant horizon, the undulating prairie, a flowering meadow of great fertility, clothed in grasses, watered by numerous streams, the margins of which was skirted in timber. . . . During Fall and Winter, the weather is usually dry. The heat of Summer is tempered by the prairie winds, and the nights are cool and comfortable. The Winters are short, dry and invigorating, with but little snow. Cold weather seldom lasts beyond three months."[5]

Outright fraud and deception were also used to market the West. The financial firm of Jay Cooke & Company, which was bankrolling the construction of the Northern Pacific line, concocted an advertising campaign of lies

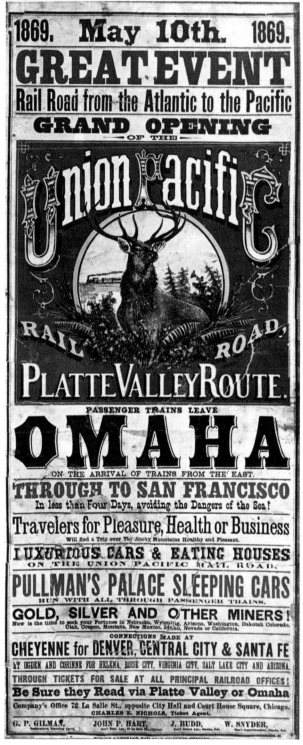

Poster for the Union Pacific

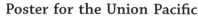

Cottontail rabbit on the plains

about the weather on the Great Plains. It was, they claimed, a land of rich soil, virgin forests, and a mild climate. Indeed, the winters were so mild, the campaign stated, that orange groves were bountiful there. People began calling the region "Jay Cooke's Banana Belt."[6]

Others attempted to mask the true climate of the Great Plains, which was wild and unpredictable, with cold winters, hot summers, and periods of drought. Since the years before the coming of the railroads had been wetter than usual, they claimed that the climate was actually changing because of the march of civilization. Plowing dirt, stringing telegraph wires, and making noise such as blowing train whistles were said to be making it rain more.

Some officials from the railroads took their claims all the way to Washington, D.C. They asked the U.S. Geological Survey to change its description of the plains from "semi-aridity" to "semi-humidity."

The Northern Pacific Railroad had hundreds of agents scattered throughout Europe, distributing literature about the Great Plains. Foreign countries or regions in which there was drought or bad soil conditions were particular targets, since it was easier to persuade people suffering hardships at home to head to a new land where everything was supposedly perfect.

New York City was the major arrival point for immigrants coming to the United States. The western railroads placed agents there whose sole job was to nab foreigners departing their boats and convince them to go west. The agents offered special immigrant rates if the newcomers rode their train lines, and they offered "advice" about where to settle and tips for farming this new land. Competition among agents was fierce.

As these new people moved in, others were forced out. There wasn't room for everyone in the development of the West—as Native Americans and the buffalo soon found out.

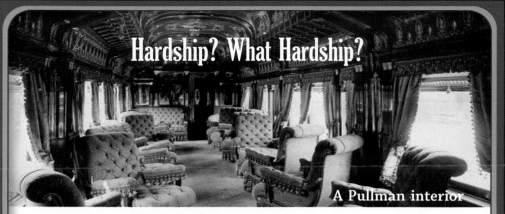

Hardship? What Hardship?

A Pullman interior

Covered wagons? Bad weather? Hostile Native American attacks? No food? Those hardships seemed light-years away from traveling west via railroad, and in particular, traveling in a Pullman car.

George M. Pullman was born on March 3, 1831, in Brocton, New York. After sleeping in his train seat, Pullman was inspired to develop a better car for passenger comfort. His first car was called the *Pioneer*. In 1865, after president Abraham Lincoln was assassinated, Pullman arranged to have the body transported to Illinois from Washington, D.C., via the *Pioneer*. Both Pullman and the car gained national attention, and railroads began ordering Pullman sleeper cars.

The luxurious sleeper cars featured hinged seats and seat backs that could be lowered to give passengers someplace to sleep at night. With their rich brown exteriors, hand-carved paneling, plush upholstery, and extravagant luxuries like libraries and card tables, the Pullman Palace cars were a hit. Even running three Pullman cars per train wasn't enough, and the Union Pacific had to turn away passenger requests for the cars. The Pullman cars were longer and wider than any built at that time, and their immense popularity forced railroads to set their station platforms and other structures back from the tracks so the cars had room to pass.

However, Pullman wasn't through. In 1867 he introduced the *Delmonico*, named after a famous New York City restaurant. The *Delmonico* was a luxury dining car that served fine cuisine, all attended by a fleet of waiters. Among the fare served was blue-winged teal (a type of duck), antelope steaks, roast beef, boiled ham and tongue, broiled chicken, corn on the cob, fresh fruit, hot rolls, cornbread, and fresh trout. No wonder Pullman passengers often reported a weight gain!

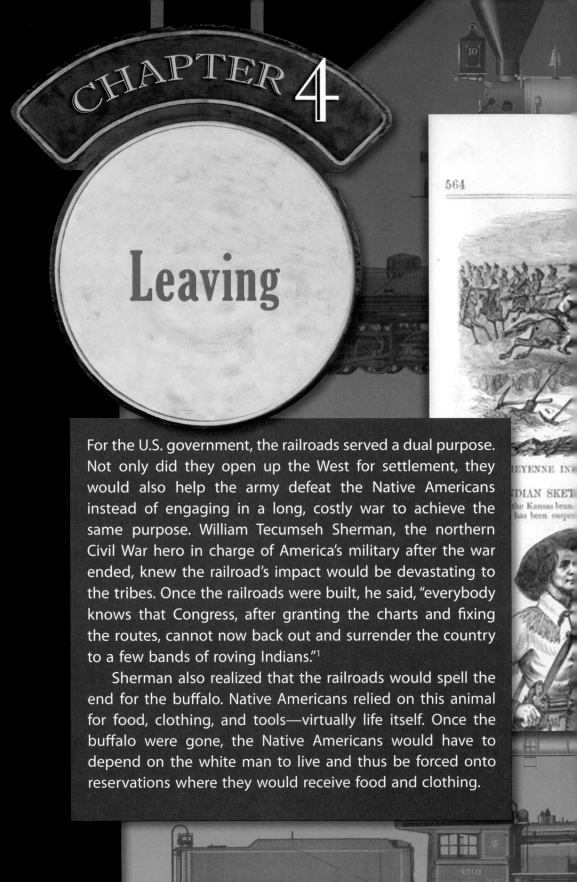

CHAPTER 4

Leaving

564

EYENNE IN

DIAN SKET
the Kansas bran
has been suspen

For the U.S. government, the railroads served a dual purpose. Not only did they open up the West for settlement, they would also help the army defeat the Native Americans instead of engaging in a long, costly war to achieve the same purpose. William Tecumseh Sherman, the northern Civil War hero in charge of America's military after the war ended, knew the railroad's impact would be devastating to the tribes. Once the railroads were built, he said, "everybody knows that Congress, after granting the charts and fixing the routes, cannot now back out and surrender the country to a few bands of roving Indians."[1]

Sherman also realized that the railroads would spell the end for the buffalo. Native Americans relied on this animal for food, clothing, and tools—virtually life itself. Once the buffalo were gone, the Native Americans would have to depend on the white man to live and thus be forced onto reservations where they would receive food and clothing.

4501

KING A WORKING PARTY ON THE UNION PACIFIC RAILROAD, AUGUST 4, 1867.—[SKETCHED BY T. R. DAVIS.]

States troops are lying idle in small squads in insecure forts; General CUSTER has marched and countermarched himself into arrest; General HANCOCK has been ordered to other duty; the Peace Commissioners are busy in blaming HANCOCK for inactivity; and General SHERMAN, in his usual original and elegant style, insists on declaring that the Commission is a "humbug." Every savage who is killed is found with at least twenty white scalps in his belt; and we are mournfully reminded while we gaze on his inanimate body that it cost one hundred thousand dollars to kill him! From every part of the frontier comes up the cry of distress; from every other part of the country are heard only the growls of dissatisfaction.

Our engravings this week will give the reader an idea of the circumstances under which the Union Pacific Railroad is being built. The "group of workmen" labor not merely with picks and spades; "Springfields" and "bowies" are a part of their working materials; and sentinels and guards are as necessary ... the road over the plains as are ... gineers. The sketch of the atta... ennes on a party of these workm... ... illustrate how the tedious ...

that would think that way ought to have corporals stripes"

In addition to our other interesting matter we give also on this page a portrait of our artist, Mr. THEODORE R. DAVIS, in his Plains costume. Mr. DAVIS has been a traveling correspondent of the

Monitor and Merrimac; the conflict at Shiloh; the capture of Corinth; the first bombardment of Vicksburg by PORTER; the battle of Antietam; the surrender of Vicksburg; the seizure of Morris Island; the battle of Chickamauga; the siege and battle of Chattanooga; the At-

Harper's Weekly was a prominent magazine that covered a lot of the news concerning the railroads, including attacks by native peoples on the work crews.

The Plum Creek Attack

To try and save their culture and thus their lives, Native Americans attacked railroad construction gangs and then the trains themselves. One of the worst attacks was the Plum Creek Attack on August 12, 1867. Under cover of darkness some warriors placed several crossties and a boulder on the tracks. When the locomotive hit this obstruction, it fell off the tracks and turned onto its side. The first four cars behind the engine piled on top of the locomotive, killing the fireman and mortally wounding the engineer. The warriors looted the broken train and did not leave until run off by soldiers. Later it was discovered that a telegraph repair crew that had gone out just before the crash had been attacked, and three men killed.

Tribes such as the Cheyenne and the Sioux, under the leadership of chiefs such as Red Cloud, Crazy Horse, and Sitting Bull, banded together after the U.S. Army slaughtered hundreds of Cheyenne and Arapaho at Sand Creek (Colorado) in 1864. The high point of their fight against advancing civilization came on June 25, 1876, when they destroyed George Armstrong Custer and his command at the Battle of the Little Bighorn, or what is often called "Custer's Last Stand." Ironically, their greatest triumph was also the beginning of the end for them. Within months the American military had driven Sitting Bull into Canada and hounded Crazy Horse until he surrendered and brought his starving band of followers into an Indian agency. Shortly after his arrival, he was stabbed in a guardhouse and died.

Even after forming strong alliances, the Native Americans were essentially powerless against the railroad. As the tracks relentlessly stretched deeper into their territory, they resigned themselves to the end of their way of life.

"As they lost more and more land, they also lost their wealth and dignity," wrote historian Sarah H. Gordon. "They began turning up at railroad stations to sit idly or to beg, or to ride the train."[2]

Ultimately all the native peoples who had lived on the western lands for centuries were crowded out by the tide of settlers brought by the railroads, and by the laws and bounties that targeted them. A Crow chief named Iron Bull said, "We have reached the end of our rule and a new one has come. The end of our lives, too, is near at hand. . . . Of our once powerful nation there are now but a few left—just a handful—and we, too, will soon be gone. After the Indian has given way to civilization the whites will come."[3]

The buffalo were another group whose presence stood in the way of the development of the West and had to go. Just after the Civil War, it is estimated there were about 15 million buffalo in North America.[4] They ranged between Canada and the Gulf coast, and when they galloped, the ground rumbled and shook as if by an earthquake. Sometimes it took hours for a herd to pass by.

Buffalo meat became a prime source of nourishment for the railroad construction crews. At the same time, demand in the eastern United States was skyrocketing for buffalo robes and buffalo tongues, a delicacy in restaurants. Buffalo bones were ground up and used as fertilizer.

Buffalo hunting to provide these items became a major source of income for many. Hunters such as William "Buffalo Bill" Cody, James Butler "Wild Bill" Hickok, and William Barclay "Bat" Masterson made their living killing buffalo. According to one estimate, almost 4 million buffalo were killed between 1871 and 1874.[5]

As the trains pushed west, railroad lines began advertising the "fun" of shooting buffalo from the windows of a train. Buffalo killing became

Railroad men shoot buffalo

a type of sport. When railroad passengers encountered a herd of buffalo they would shoot them down from the train. There was no limit on killing them, so passengers would gun down the animals until they ran out of bullets or their guns got too hot. "Everybody runs out and commences shooting," said a train traveler.[6] In some cases, Gatling guns (the forerunner of machine guns) were used to mow down several animals at a time. The result of this wanton killing was a landscape full of rotting carcasses and sun-bleached bones, as the huge animals were simply left to lie where they had been cut down. In dismay, Native American tribes watched their major source of food get exterminated.

The building of the Union Pacific Railroad across the Great Plains split the great buffalo herd into two—a northern and a southern herd. By the end of 1875, the southern herd had been virtually annihilated, and in a few more years the northern herd followed suit. Just as General Sherman had foreseen, the destruction of the buffalo hastened the demise of the native peoples as well.

"These men have done more in the last two years, and will do more in the next year, to settle the vexed Indian question, than the entire regular army has done in the last forty years," said General Philip Sheridan of the buffalo hunters.[7]

The West was about to be settled. For that to happen, the Native Americans and the buffalo had to go—and go they did.

Train Robbers

Trains brought lasting change. They also brought something else—train robbers.

The first armed hold up of a Central Pacific train occurred on November 5, 1870. It happened in the early hours of the morning on-board the eastbound express *No. 1* from Oakland to Ogden, Utah. Just outside of Verdi, Nevada (near Reno), a man hopped into the engine cab, pointed two pistols at the startled crew, and ordered the train to be brought to a halt. Once it stopped, passengers from the coach got out and disconnected the coach from the rest of the train. Once the engine and express car were free, it chugged off into the darkness.

Next the gang of six bandits burst into the express car, tied up the unarmed express agent, and broke open the safe. Inside was $41,600 in gold coins, and thousands more in currency and gold dust. The bandits took it all, then had the engine move to within a few miles of Reno. Here the robbers left the train and vanished into the night.

Unfortunately for the crooks, the rest of their plan did not go as well. All six were caught within a week. They all wound up with prison sentences. Thereafter, an armed guard rode with express trains carrying a large amount of cash.

It took several more years for the Union Pacific to suffer its first robbery. On the night of August 27, 1875, two men climbed onto the roof of the express car, then lowered themselves down the side of the train car via ropes and got into the express car through an unlocked window. While the express agent slept, the men unclipped his key ring from his pocket and unlocked the strongbox. The messenger awoke, and the bandits started shooting. Fortunately none of their bullets hit anything. By this time the train was reaching a station and began slowing down. The bandits fled into the night, having only taken a few items not worth much money.

These were the first robberies on the transcontinental lines, but they wouldn't be the last.

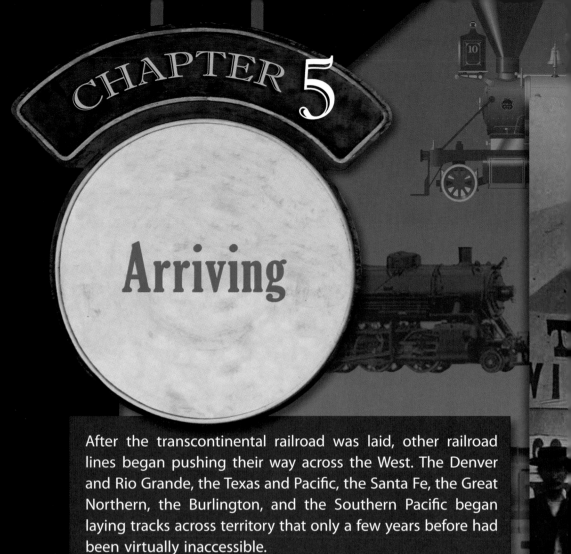

CHAPTER 5

Arriving

After the transcontinental railroad was laid, other railroad lines began pushing their way across the West. The Denver and Rio Grande, the Texas and Pacific, the Santa Fe, the Great Northern, the Burlington, and the Southern Pacific began laying tracks across territory that only a few years before had been virtually inaccessible.

Sometimes, however, development was not meant to be permanent. As the railroad workers got paid and sought enjoyment, they found little on which to spend their money on the vast open plains. Thus came the infamous "Hell on Wheels"—temporary cities of canvas or wood that shadowed the railroad crews and were filled with prostitution, gambling, drinking, and any other activity likely to separate a man from his money.

As railroad historian John Hoyt Williams wrote of the encampments: "Drunken trackmen blended with painted whores, knife-wielding pimps, and shifty, Derringer-toting gamblers to form a brew more volatile than Red Dog [a one-

As the railroad pushed west, towns sprang up almost overnight on land that had been vacant for centuries. Some of these towns lasted for only a few months, as the railroad moved on and the town's reason for existence vanished.

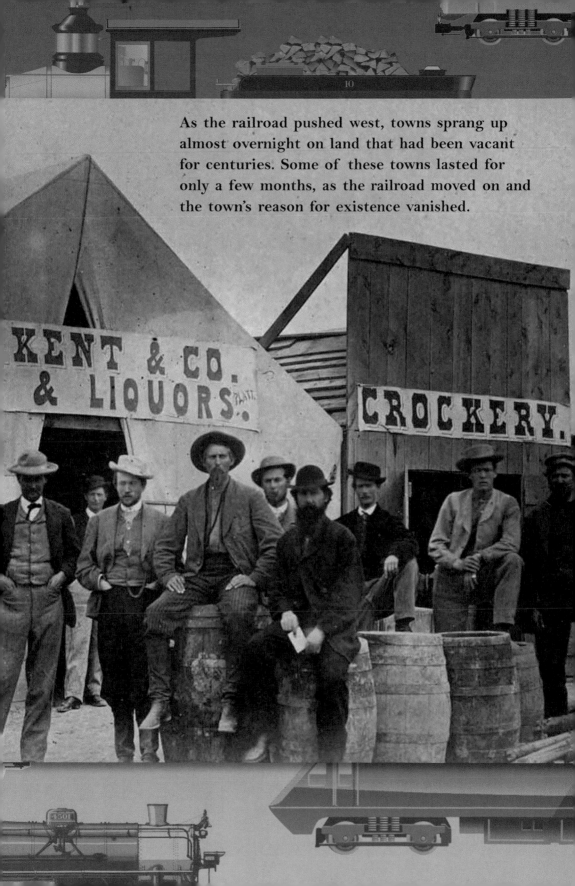

hundred-proof liquor], and one even more prone to explode. The result was a trail of hangovers, bruises and contusions, festering sores, and corpses stretching out behind the Union Pacific like survey stakes."[1]

Permanent towns also followed the tracks, popping up all over the West like weeds after a summer rain. One minute there was nothing but open space; the next there was a town. At one site in Wyoming, a train filled with everything from tents and lumber to billiard tables and pianos pulled up. The conductor got off the train, waved his hand at the cars filled with goods, and announced: "Gentlemen, here's [the town of] Julesburg."[2]

Western states and cities boomed. The population of Nebraska soared to over a million people in just about twenty years thanks to the railroads. In a little over twenty years, Omaha went from being a small town to a major meatpacking center for the entire country.

Sometimes western development could be unpredictable. In late 1877, Garland City in Colorado was made a railroad terminus (last stop). Within two weeks it contained 105 houses. There was a roar of noise as workmen cut, hammered, and hollered, throwing buildings up in the hastily built town.

As the railroad progressed farther west, a new terminus was established. There was no more need for Garland City, so it was completely torn down.

Towns vied furiously with each other to become a stop on the train line. A stop meant that people and cargo would come and go, and the town would grow. Locations that were bypassed by the railroad ran the risk of withering and dying.

Towns could also bid on spurs that would connect them to the main tracks. Connecting their town to the vast national rail network seemed a surefire way to bring in cash, so they would borrow heavily to pay for one. Many towns went bankrupt this way.

Millions of people journeyed west by rail to start over in this suddenly accessible region. Migration to the West via the railroad took all shapes and forms. Orphan trains organized by the New York

Children without homes or families were shipped west on trains, where they hoped to be adopted or at least chosen by western families to begin a new life with them. This enterprise is now recognized as the beginning of foster care in the United States.

Children's Aid Society took abandoned and orphaned children to the West. Once they arrived, farm families and other interested people looked over the newly transplanted children, picking out which ones they wanted to adopt. Ninety thousand children were shipped west on these trains.[3]

People had individual reasons for going west. Some came for a fresh start, but others treated the region as a new country for their children to grow up in and enjoy. However, like many of the settlers when they arrived, they found the truth was something different from the railroad's rosy pictures of the Great Plains. They found a land in which everything but earth and sky was scarce. Water was so precious that it often had to be hauled in barrels from miles away, or coaxed from wells hundreds of feet deep. Flash floods, tornadoes, and intense heat were often the weather feature of the day—sometimes in the same day. The land was so barren of trees that houses had to be made of sod, and fuel was whatever could be found—even buffalo chips.

Yet still they came west . . . farmers, settlers, merchants, gold seekers, the determined and the just plain curious. They were all part of one of

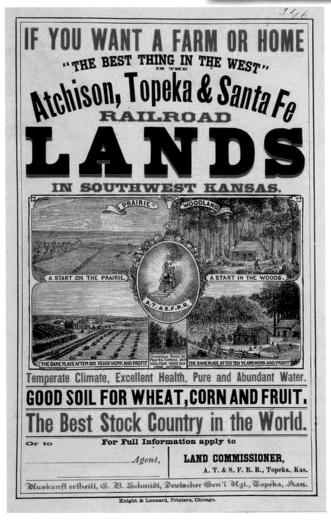

Atchison, Topeka and Santa Fe Railroad
poster

the greatest mass migrations in recorded history—the settling of the American West. Everyone knew something important for the future of the country had been done with the opening of the West by rail. Many people came by way of the first transcontinental railroad, but other railroads to the West were also built over the next several decades that also brought passengers by the thousands into once-desolate areas. The Southern Pacific built a line from Southern California to New Orleans, while the Atchison, Topeka and Santa Fe line ran from Kansas to southern California. Both the Northern Pacific and the Great Northern ran from Minnesota to Seattle and other northern points along the West Coast. They were coming to a region that once had been a prime example of the wide open spaces. Thanks to the railroads, the lonely call of the prairie dog had been replaced by the buzzing of saws and the pounding of hammers as buildings filled in the once-vast emptiness.

The Day of the Two Noons

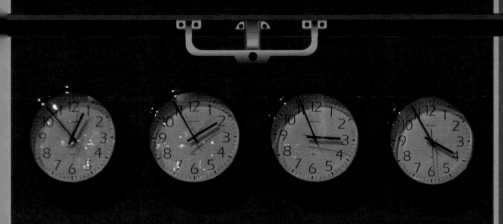

Before the railroads, people in the United States lived primarily by the sun. They worked their farms when it was light, and went to bed when it was dark. "Local time" was determined by each particular place—it could be 10:00 in the morning in one place, 9:20 in another place, and so on.

However, the railroads could not operate like that. It would hardly do for a train to leave a station at one time, and then arrive at its destination earlier than when it left. Thus the railroads needed a uniform system of time.

They hired New Jersey resident William F. Allen to solve their problem. Allen had been the editor of a magazine dealing with railway and steamship timetables, so he was familiar with travel schedules and time problems. He decided to divide the country into four different time zones. Wherever possible, he followed existing state and territorial boundaries, which made the system easier for people to use. Noon in each zone would be marked when the sun was at its highest at a certain degree of longitude.

The railroads accepted Allen's time scheme in October 1883. With great fanfare, Sunday, November 18, 1883, became the "Day of the Two Noons." At 12:28 p.m. on that day, each railroad clock was turned back to twelve noon as noon was reached in their particular time zone.

Faced with being either in step with the railroads or not, most of the rest of the country replaced their local time with standard time. It would be another thirty-five years, however, before Congress enacted standard time.

1800	The U.S. capital is moved from Philadelphia to Washington, D.C.
1803	The Louisiana Purchase doubles the size of the United States.
1815	Napoleon is defeated at Waterloo.
1825	The Erie Canal, connecting Lake Erie with the Hudson River, is completed.
1830	After the Indian Removal Act is passed, Cherokee, Chickasaw, Muscogee (Creek), Seminole, and Choctaw nations, among others, are forced to march west from their southeastern lands; thousands of them die in what will come to be known as the Trail of Tears.
1835	Texas declares independence from Mexico.
1846	After Mexico's defeat in the Mexican-American War, the United States gains New Mexico and Alta, California.
1852	*Uncle Tom's Cabin* is published, revealing the negative impact that slavery has on Southern families.
1860	Abraham Lincoln is elected sixteenth President of the United States.
1861	The Civil War begins.
1865	The first Chinese immigrants are employed by the Central Pacific Railroad to build the transcontinental railroad. Slavery is abolished; the Civil War ends; Lincoln is assassinated.
1866	Dynamite is invented; black powder continues to be used in railroad construction.
1869	The first transcontinental railroad, joining Omaha, Nebraska, to San Francisco, California, is completed on May 10.
1870	On August 15, the first continuous railway from the Atlantic Ocean (New York) to the Pacific Ocean (San Francisco) is joined at Comanche Crossing in Strasburg, Colorado. The Fifteenth Amendment to the U.S. Constitution is ratified, giving African-Americans the right to vote.
1870	The first internal combustion engine using liquid gasoline is invented.
1875	The southern buffalo herd has been virtually wiped out.
1876	Cheyenne and Sioux forces destroy George Armstrong Custer and his command at the Battle of the Little Bighorn.
1878	Andrew Chase designs a railroad car that can keep meat cold for long distances, eliminating the need to transport livestock and drastically reducing food loss and per-unit shipping costs.
1882	William F. Cody creates the traveling show Buffalo Bill's Wild West.
1883	Railroads adopt five time zones for the United States and Canada, implementing standardized time.
1886	Southern railroad companies adopt the standard gauge (4 feet, 8.5 inches) for their rail lines.
1886	Henry Ford builds his first automobile.
1890	At the Battle of Wounded Knee in South Dakota, the U.S. 7th Cavalry massacres dozens of Lakota Sioux men, women, and children.
1898	The United States defeats Spain in the Spanish-American War, gaining the Philippine Islands, Puerto Rico, and Guam; Cuba also gains independence from Spain.
1903	The Wright brothers make the first powered flight in Kitty Hawk, North Carolina.
1908	General Motors is formed.

Chapter 1. Go West—By Railroad
1. John Hoyt Williams, *A Great & Shining Road* (New York: Times Books, 1988), p. 262.
2. Sarah Gordon, *Passage to Union* (Chicago: Ivan R. Dee, 1996), p. 14.
3. Russell Roberts and Rich Youmans, *Down the Jersey Shore* (New Brunswick, New Jersey: Rutgers University Press, 1993), p. 26.
4. Sarah Gordon, *Passage to Union* (Chicago: Ivan R. Dee, 1996), p. 15.
5. Robert Selph Henry. *Trains* (Indianapolis, Indiana: The Bobbs- Merrill Company,1949), p. 11.
6. Dee Brown, *Hear that Lonesome Whistle Blow* (New York: Holt, Rinehart and Winston, 1977), p. 28.
7. Keith Wheeler, *The Old West—The Railroaders* (New York: Time-Life Books, 1973), p. 19.
8. The History Channel, "The Transcontinental Railroad," 1995.

Chapter 2. Spanning a Continent
1. The History Channel, "The Transcontinental Railroad," 1995.
2. John Hoyt Williams, *A Great & Shining Road* (New York: Times Books, 1988), p. 72.
3. Gerald M. Best, *Iron Horses to Promontory* (San Marino, California: Golden West Books, 1969), p. 12.
4. Keith Wheeler, *The Old West—The Railroaders* (New York: Time-Life Books, 1973), p. 72.
5. Ibid., p. 98.
6. The History Channel, "The Transcontinental Railroad," 1995.
7. Dee Brown, Hear that Lonesome Whistle Blow (New York: Holt, Rinehart and Winston, 1977), p. 74.
8. Stephen E. Ambrose, Nothing Like It in the World (New York: Simon & Schuster, 2000), p. 150.
9. 7. Dee Brown, *Hear that Lonesome Whistle Blow* (New York: Holt, Rinehart and Winston, 1977), p. 76.
10. John Hoyt Williams, *A Great & Shining Road* (New York: Times Books, 1988), p. 263.
11. S. Mintz, "Chinese Immigrants and the Building of the Transcontinental Railroad," *Digital History,* 2007, http://www.digitalhistory.uh.edu/historyonline/china1.cfm
12. Gerald M. Best, *Iron Horses to Promontory* (San Marino, California: Golden West Books, 1969), p. 55.

Chapter 3. The Railroads Sell the West
1. Keith Wheeler, *The Old West—The Railroaders* (New York: Time-Life Books, 1973), p. 135.
2. Ibid, p. 135.
3. Dee Brown, *The American West* (New York: Charles Scribner's Sons, 1994), p. 136.
4. Page Smith, *The Rise of Industrial America—Volume Six* (New York: McGraw-Hill Book Company, 1984), p. 99.
5. Sarah Gordon, *Passage to Union* (Chicago: Ivan R. Dee, 1996), p. 159.
6. Oliver Jensen, *The American Heritage History of Railroads In America* (New York: American Heritage Publishing Co. Inc, 1975), p. 107.

Chapter 4. Leaving
1. Stephen E. Ambrose, *Crazy Horse and Custer: The Parallel Lives of Two American Warriors* (New York: Anchor Books, 1996), p. 275.
2. Sarah H. Gordon, *Passage to Union* (Chicago: Ivan R. Dee, 1996), p. 155.

3. Page Smith, *The Rise of Industrial America—Volume Six* (New York: McGraw-Hill Book Company, 1984), p. 95.
4. Allan Nevins, *The Emergence of Modern America 1865–1878* (New York: The MacMillan Company, 1928), p. 112.
5. Ibid, p. 113.
6. Dee Brown, *Hear that Lonesome Whistle Blow* (New York: Holt, Rinehart and Winston, 1977), p. 145.
7. Kathy Weiser, "Old West Legends: Buffalo Hunters," Legends of America, August 2011, http://legendsofamerica.com/we-buffalohunters.html

Chapter 5. Arriving
1. John Hoyt Williams, *A Great & Shining Road* (New York: Times Books, 1988), p. 127.
2. Oliver Jensen, *The American Heritage History of Railroads In America* (New York: American Heritage Publishing Co. Inc, 1975), p. 105.
3. Thomas J. Schlereth, *Victorian America* (New York: HarperCollins Publishers, 1991), p. 13.
4. Dee Brown, *The American West* (New York: Charles Scribner's Sons, 1994), p. 136.
5. Thomas Fuller, " 'Go West, Young Man'—An Elusive Slogan," *Indiana Magazine of History,* September 2004, http://www.jstor.org/pss/27792556

Works Consulted

Ambrose, Stephen E. *Crazy Horse and Custer.* New York: Anchor Books, 1996.

Ambrose, Stephen E. *Nothing Like It in the World.* New York: Simon & Schuster, 2000.

Best, Gerald M. *Iron Horses to Promontory.* San Marino, California: Golden West Books, 1969.

Brown, Dee. *The American West.* New York: Charles Scribner's Sons, 1994.

Brown, Dee. *Hear that Lonesome Whistle Blow.* New York: Holt, Rinehart and Winston, 1977.

"From Rail to Trail." *Southern Pacific Bulletin,* monthly installments, 1926–1928.
    http://cprr.org/Museum/Southern_Pacific_Bulletin/index.html

Fuller, Thomas. " 'Go West, Young Man'—An Elusive Slogan." *Indiana Magazine of History,* September 2004. http://www.jstor.org/pss/27792556

Gordon, Sarah. *Passage to Union.* Chicago, Illinois: Ivan R. Dee, 1996.

Henry, Robert Selph. *Trains.* Indianapolis, Indiana: The Bobbs- Merrill Company, 1949.

Jensen, Oliver. *The American Heritage History of Railroads In America.* New York: American Heritage Publishing Co. Inc., 1975.

Merk, Frederick. *History of the Westward Movement.* New York: Alfred A. Knopf, 1978.

Mintz, S. "Chinese Immigrants and the Building of the Transcontinental Railroad." Digital History, 2007.

Nevins, Allan. *The Emergence of Modern America 1865–1878.* New York: The MacMillan Company, 1928.

Roberts, Russell, and Rich Youmans. *Down the Jersey Shore.* New Brunswick, New Jersey: Rutgers University Press, 1993.

Schlereth, Thomas J. *Victorian America.* New York: HarperCollins Publishers, 1991.

Works Consulted

Works Consulted

Smith, Page. *The Rise of Industrial America—Volume Six*. New York: McGraw-Hill Book Company, 1984.

Strobridge, Edson T. "Building the Central Pacific Roadbed Around Cape Horn." *Central Pacific Railroad Photographic Museum*. http://cprr.org/Museum/Cape_Horn.html#1886

The Transcontinental Railroad—The History Channel, 1995.

Wheeler, Keith. *The Old West—The Railroaders*. New York: Time-Life Books, 1973.

Wheeler, Keith. *The Old West—The Townsmen*. New York: Time-Life Books, 1975.

Williams, John Hoyt. *A Great & Shining Road*. New York: Times Books, 1988.

FURTHER READING

Books

Alfred, Randy. "Nov. 18, 1883: Railroad Time Goes Coast to Coast." *Wired,* November 18, 2010. http://www.wired.com/thisdayintech/tag/william-f-allen/

Arnosky, Jim. *Grandfather Buffalo*. New York: Putnam Juvenile, 2006.

Cunningham, Kevin, and Peter Benoit. *The Sioux*. San Francisco: Children's Press, 2011.

Evans, Clark J. *The Central Pacific Railroad*. San Francisco: Children's Press, 2007.

Patent, Dorothy Hinshaw, and William Munoz. *The Buffalo and the Indians: A Shared Destiny*. New York: Clarion Books, 2006.

Stanley, George Edward. *Sitting Bull: Great Sioux Hero*. New York: Sterling, 2010.

Uschan, Michael V. *The Transcontinental Railroad*. Farmington Hills, Michigan: Lucent, 2009.

Shapiro, Carl, and Hal R. Varian. "History in Motion—Railroad Guages: A Standards Battle." An excerpt from Chapter 7 of *Information Rules. Railroad.net*. http://www.railroad.net/articles/columns/history/gauges/index.php

On the Internet

Central Pacific Railroad Photographic History Museum
    http://cprr.org/

Comanche Crossing Historical Society
    http://www.cchscolorado.org/

Golden Spike National Historic Site
    http://www.nps.gov/gosp/index.htm

Library of Congress—American Memory: "Railroad Maps 1828–1900
    http://rs6.loc.gov/ammem/gmdhtml/rrhtml/rrhome.html

Union Pacific Railroad Museum
    http://www.uprrmuseum.org/

U.S. History: Binding the Nation by Rail
    http://www.ushistory.org/us/36a.asp

U.S. History: Early American Railroads
    http://www.ushistory.org/us/25b.asp

advocate (AD-voh-kayt)—To speak in favor of a person, group, or plan.

aridity (ayr-IH-dih-tee)—The dryness of a region.

deed—As in a land deed, a document produced to start legal proceedings.

encroach (en-KROHCH)—To pass a boundary into someone else's area.

Gatling gun (GAT-ling GUN)—An early type of machine gun.

gauge (GAYJ)—The distance between the rails on a railroad track.

humidity (hyoo-MIH-dih-tee)—The dampness in the air.

incentive (in-SEN-tiv)—Something that causes action to be taken.

locomotive (loh-kuh-MOH-tiv)—A self-propelled vehicle for pulling trains.

longitude (LON-jih-tood) – a distance east or west on the earth's surface.

onerous (OH-nuh-rus)—Difficult, burdensome, or troublesome.

secede (seh-SEED)—To withdraw from a group, such as from the union of the United States.

terrain (tur-RAYN)—The features of a piece of land, such as its shape and texture.

venture (VEN-chur)—A project that involves chance, risk, or danger, such as starting a new business.

visionary (VIH-zuh-nayr-ee)—Someone whose ideas help improve the future.

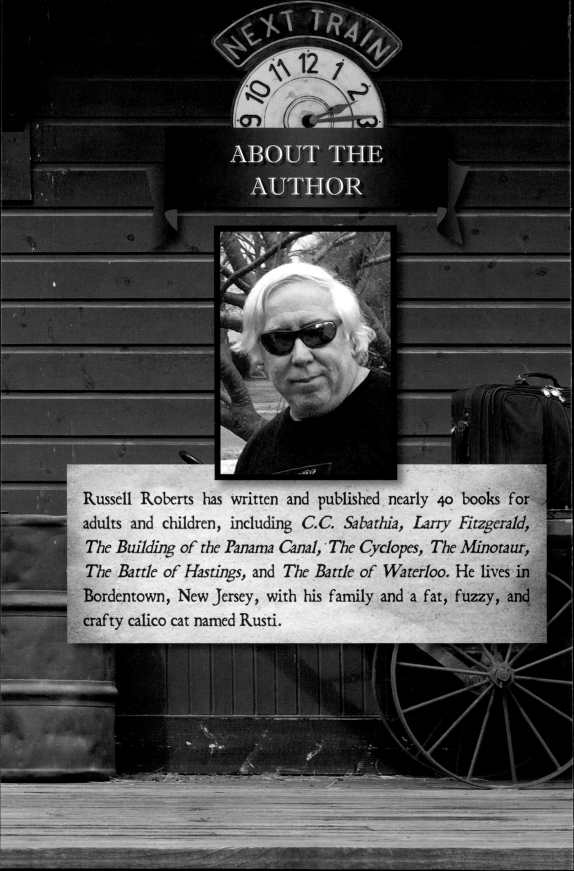

ABOUT THE
AUTHOR

Russell Roberts has written and published nearly 40 books for adults and children, including *C.C. Sabathia, Larry Fitzgerald, The Building of the Panama Canal, The Cyclopes, The Minotaur, The Battle of Hastings,* and *The Battle of Waterloo.* He lives in Bordentown, New Jersey, with his family and a fat, fuzzy, and crafty calico cat named Rusti.